BOOK 2
Revised

CREATIVE MUSIC

Robert Pace

WALTZ
(Variation 2)

1. First, play as written then transpose to E and F Major. For Creative Reading each day, change notes in the first, third, fifth and seventh measures.

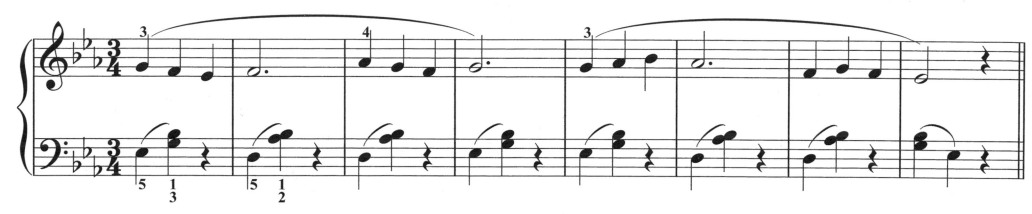

SHORT AND LIVELY

2. Play as written, then transpose to G, E and E♭ Major. Each day for Creative Reading, change the melodic patterns a little by using repeated notes, skips, or inversions.

SHORT AND LIVELY

1. For several days only create Answers to this Question. Later in the week, create your own new Questions and Answer them.

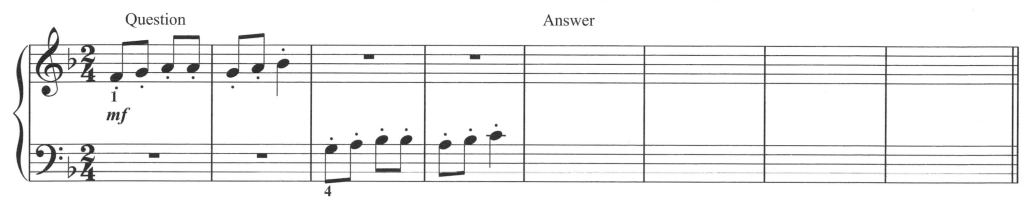

PATTERNS

2. Play this Question and Answer as written, then use this general pattern to create other Questions and Answers.

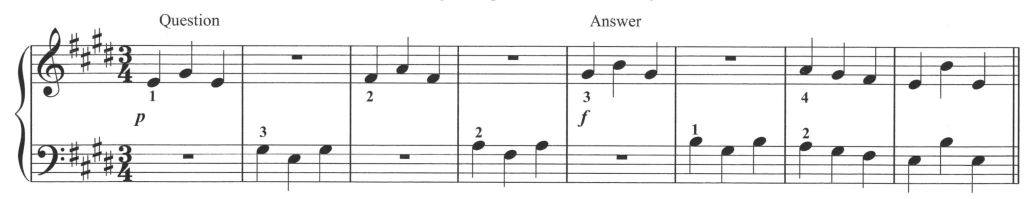

PEDAL STUDY

1. First play as written, then transpose to D and D♭ Major. For Creative Reading repeat some of the notes in the melody.
   Tranpose to E♭ ans F Major.

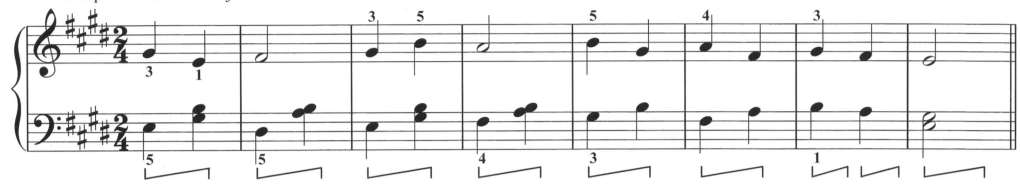

CHORD COLORS

2. For Creative Reading invert the pattern in either or both hands.

QUESTIONS AND ANSWERS

1. Create both parallel and contrasting Answers to this Question. Also, create new Questions.

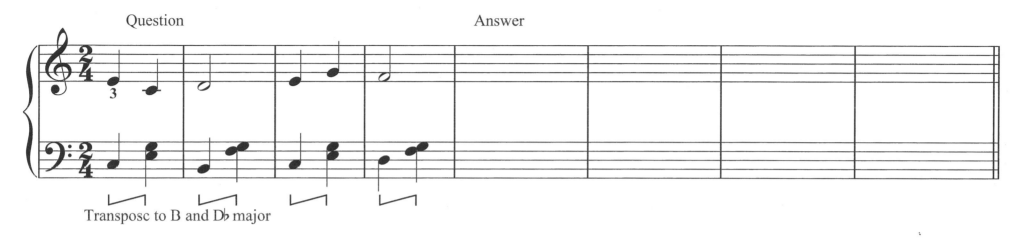

Question   Answer

Transpose to B and D♭ major

CHORD COLORS

2. After creating Answers to this Question for several days make up new Questions to Anwer. Use your pedal to get interesting harmonies.

Question   Answer

SONG

1. Keep the same notes in the bass and change the right hand melody for Creative Reading. Transpose to G♭, E and E♭.

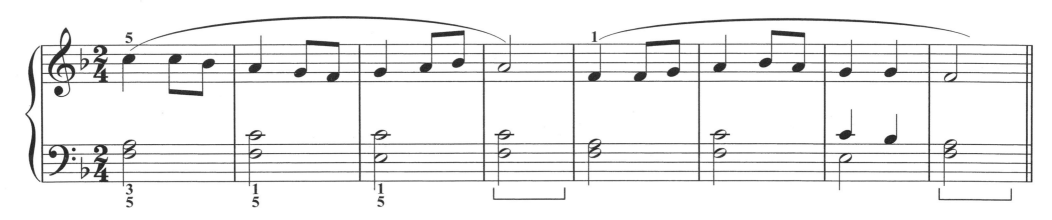

PHRYGIAN DANCE

2. Change a few notes in the melody for your Creative Reading and transpose down one step to play it in the Dorian mode.

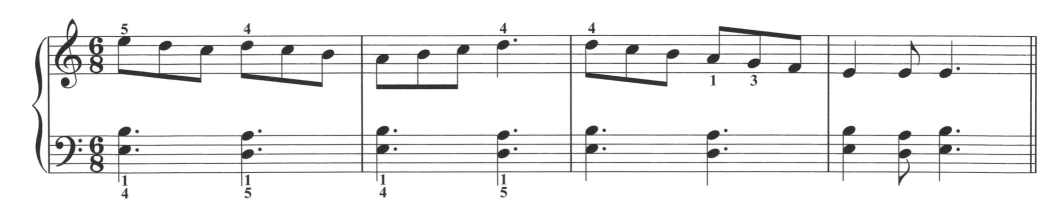

BASS MELODY

1. Here the Question is in the left hand and the harmony is in the right hand part. Your Answers can be in either hand so experiment with both.

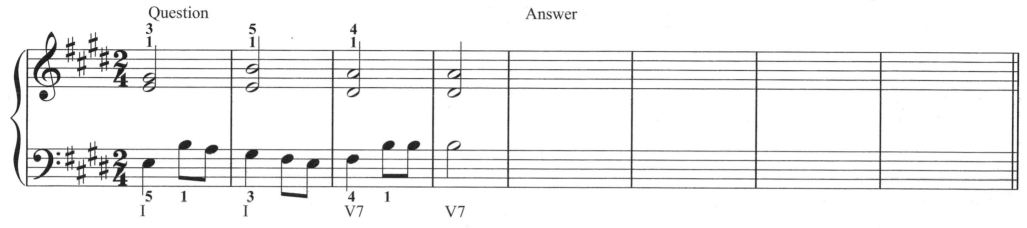

DORIAN TUNE

2. For several days create as many different Answers to this Question as possible. Then, create new Questions and Answers in Dorian mode using using skips and repeated tones.

FRÈRE JACQUES

There are many different things you can do for variety in your Creative Reading. For example, start with the right hand then let the left hand follow, or change the skips and steps in the basic patterns. Transpose to E♭, D and D♭ major.

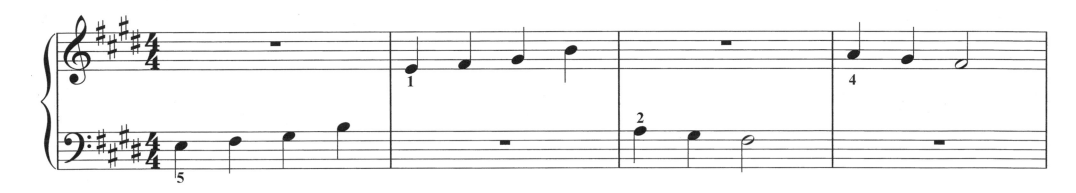

QUESTIONS AND ANSWERS

1. Create both parallel and contrasting Answers. Also, in either G or E minor, make up new Questions to Answer.

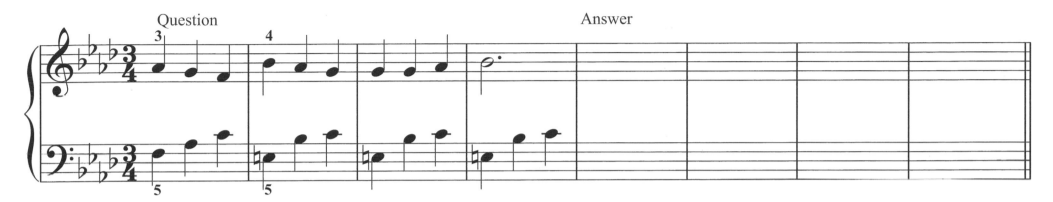

MELODIC PATTERNS

2. For the first few days, give both parallel and contrasting Answers. Later, use the same rhythm to create new Questions.

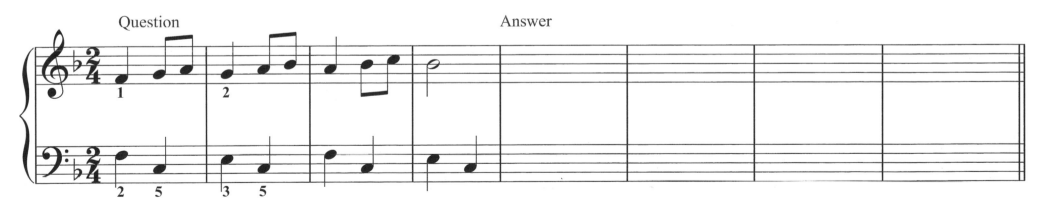

DREAMING

1. Notice that this melody is an *inversion* of the melody in *Music for Piano*, p. 10. Create new melodies for this same bass patterns.

VARIATION

2. Each day for Creative Reading create another melodic variation for this same bass pattern. Transpose to F, D and D♭ Major.

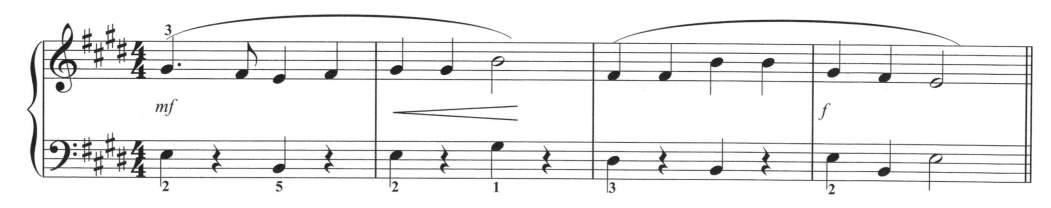

CHANGING METER

1. Create Answers with changing meter to this Question. Also create some of your own Questions to Answer.

Question

VARIATION

2. Create both parallel and contrasting Answers to this Question. Also, change the key to F minor, and create more Questions and Answers.

Question

TWELVE TONE MELODIES

1. Here is the same *row* or *series* that was used in *Music for Piano Book 2*, but with a different rhythm. Experiment with other rhythms for Creative Reading.

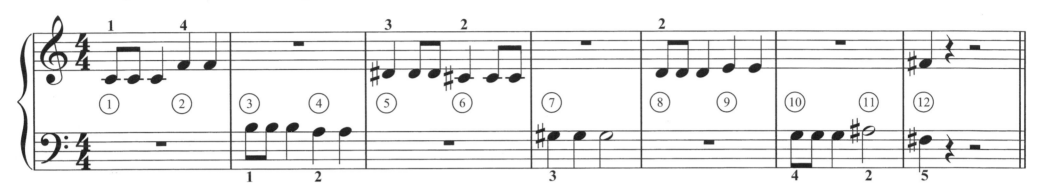

RHYTHMIC VARIATIONS

2. You may repeat the tones of the row and end on any tone. In the third and fourth measures, the first nine tones are used again, but with a different rhythm. You may also use any meter or have a changing meter if you wish.

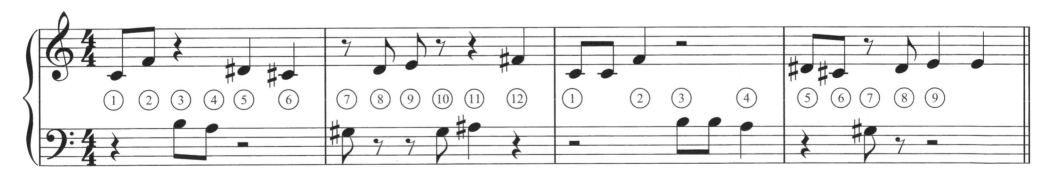

BASIC ROW

1. Here is the row from *Music for Piano*, page 12. You can create interesting Questions and Answers by
   changing the notes of the row from treble to bass and using other rhythms. You may use any part of
   the row in your Question and also in your Answer.

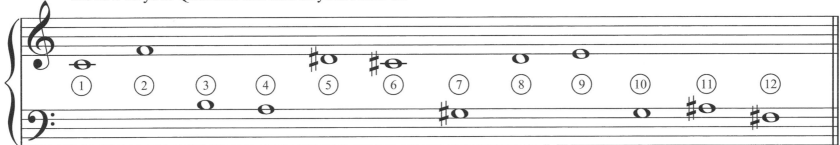

METER CHANGES

2. Here are two examples of twelve tone Questions first in $\frac{6}{8}$ meter and the other in $\frac{3}{4}$ meter.

Question   Answer

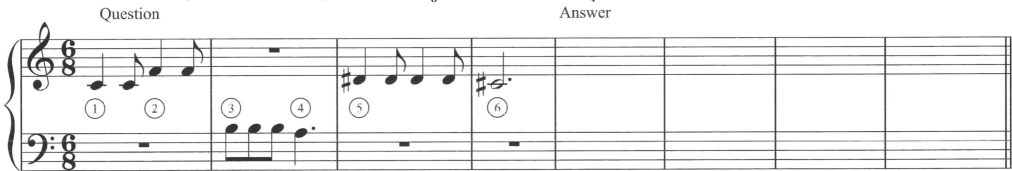

Question   Answer

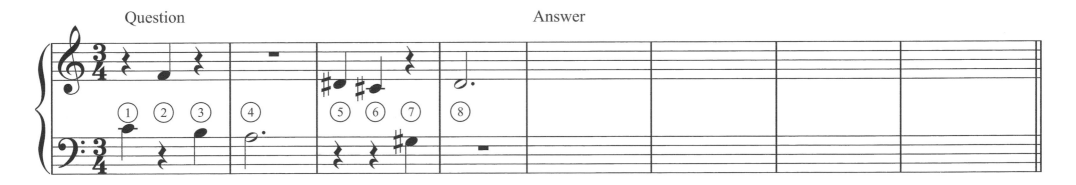

THE IV CHORD

1. Notice where the melody consists of *chord tones* and where it has *passing tones*. Notice that as you go from the I to the IV chord, the top note of the I chord moves up *one whole step* while the middle note only moves up *one half step*. Transpose to D♭, D and E Major.

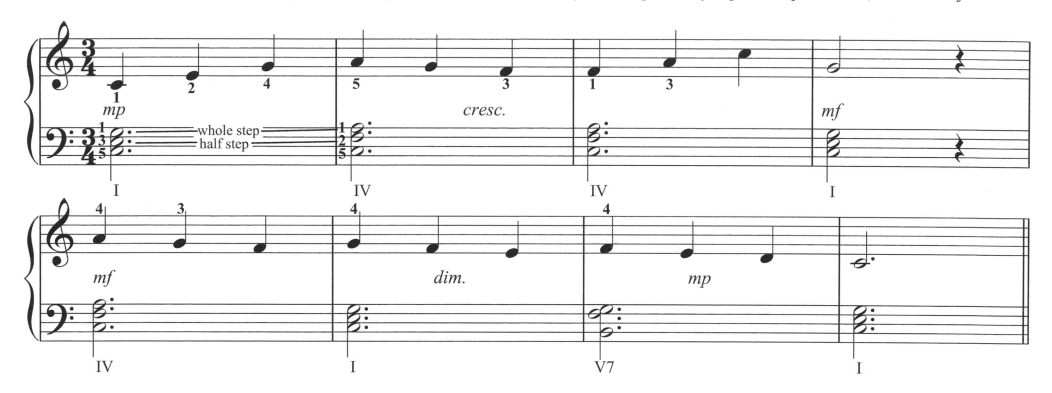

JOLLY GOOD FELLOW

2. Change the melodic patterns for Creative Reading and transpose to D♭, C and B Major.

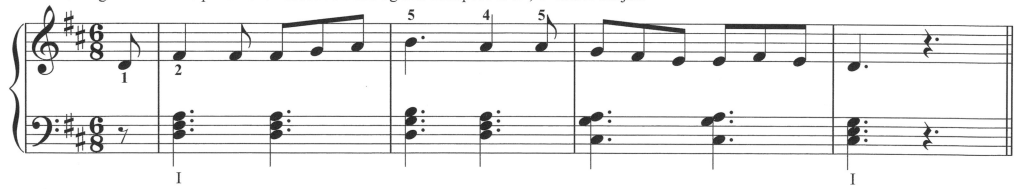

QUESTION AND ANSWER

1. Create both parallel and contrasting Answers to these Questions. Also, try different chord patterns in your new Questions.

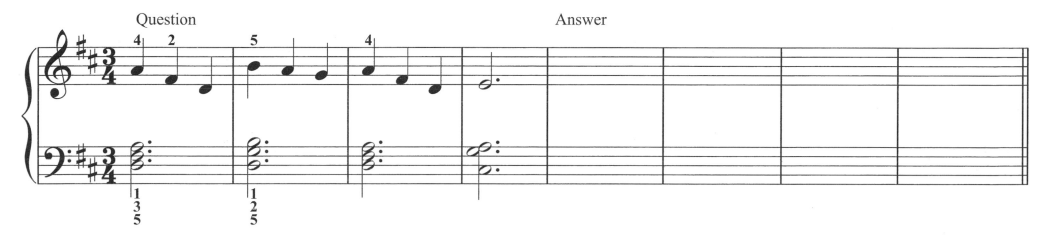

MELODIC VARIATIONS

2. After creating parallel and contrasting Answers to this Question, use the same rhythm to create more Questions and Answers.

MELODIC GROUPS

1. Notice the melodic groupings in the right hand and the steady half note pattern of the left hand. Change a few notes in the right hand for your creative reading and transpose to Db and F Major.

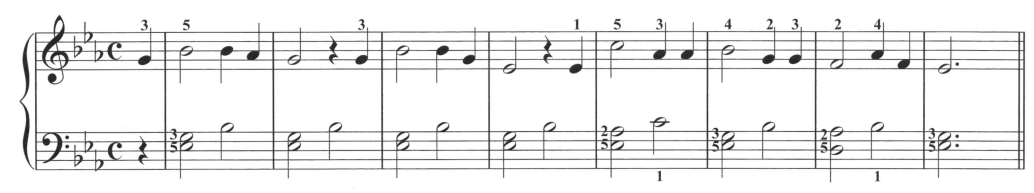

REPETITIONS AND INVERSIONS

2. Look for the repetitions and inversions in this melody. After playing as written for several days, change some of the notes in these patterns for creative reading. Transpose to D and C major.

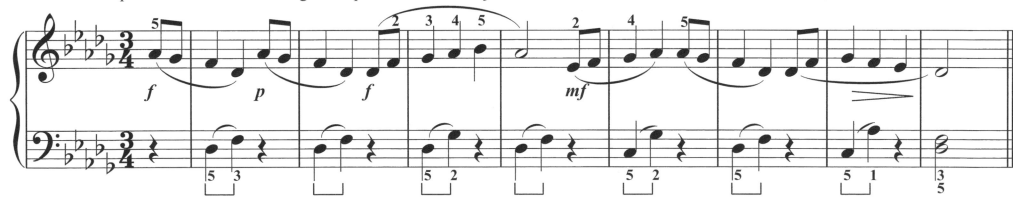

QUESTION AND ANSWER

1. Each day create new Answers to this Question. Also, you may create your own Question to Answer. Notate one of your Answers.

Question   Answer

QUESTION AND ANSWER

2. Create both parallel and contrasting Answers to this Question.

Question   Answer

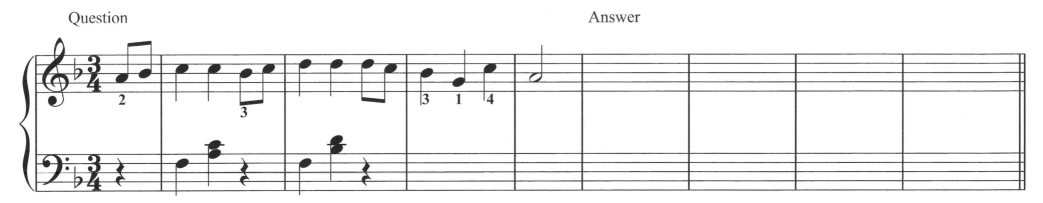

MELODIC PATTERNS

1. Look for the melodic patterns and chord changes. For Creative Reading, change a few of the notes in these patterns.
   Transpose to F and G Major.

VARIATION

2. This melody is harmonized with triads moving up and down the G Major scale. Transpose to F and A Major.

QUESTION AND ANSWER

1. Create parallel and contrasting Answers for this Question. Also make up new pentatonic Questions using only the black keys.

QUESTION AND ANSWER

2. Give both parallel and conrasting Answers to this Question. Also use the same rhythm and chord pattern to create your own Questions and Answers.

BOOGIE BLUES

1. You may change either or both parts for your Creative Reading.

PARALLEL MOTION

2. For Creative Reading invert some of the patterns. Tranpose this to F, E♭, A♭, and A Major.

BLUES QUESTION AND ANSWER

1. Keep the same bass pattern (ostinato) and each day create new Questions and Answers.

QUESTION AND ANSWER

2. Notice where the right and left hand parts move in parallel motion and where they move in contrary motion.
   You may change this for your new Questions and Answers.

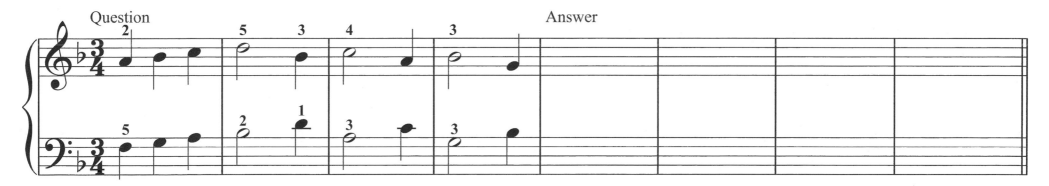

PARALLEL AND CONTRASTING MOTION

1. Make some changes in the direction of the two lines (from contrary to parallel) for Creative Reading. Transpose to C, D and E Major.

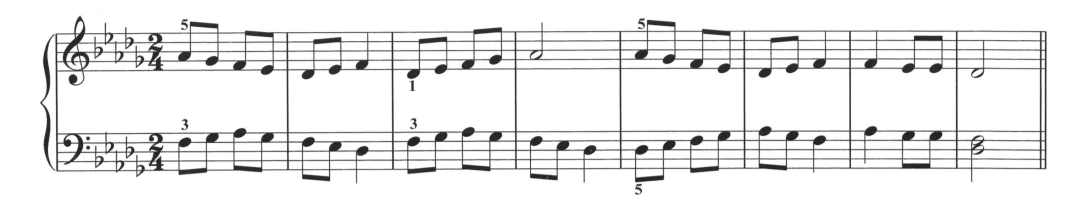

DIATONIC TRIADS

2. Each day for Creative Reading, keep the same bass pattern and create new melodies.

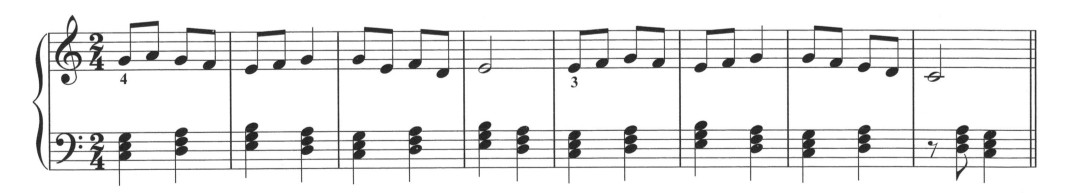

QUESTION AND ANSWER

1. Make up parallel and contrasting Answers to this Question. Also, create new Questions with different harmonic progressions
   (I IV I V7 or I IV V7 I) for example.

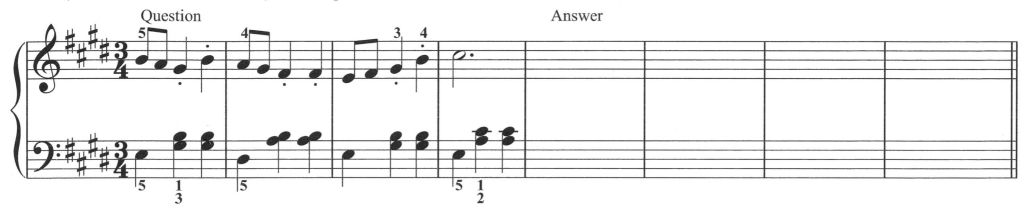

QUESTION AND ANSWER

2. You may use notes from the entire octave (C to C) as you create Answers to this Question.
   Also use the entire octave as you make up new Questions.

QUIET TIME

1. For Creative Reading make up new melodies in the Phrygian mode over this bass line.
   Tranpose down one whole step to play it in the Dorian mode.

DIATONIC TRIADS

2. Keep the same bass chords, but change the melody for Creative Reading. Transpose up one step to play this in G Major.

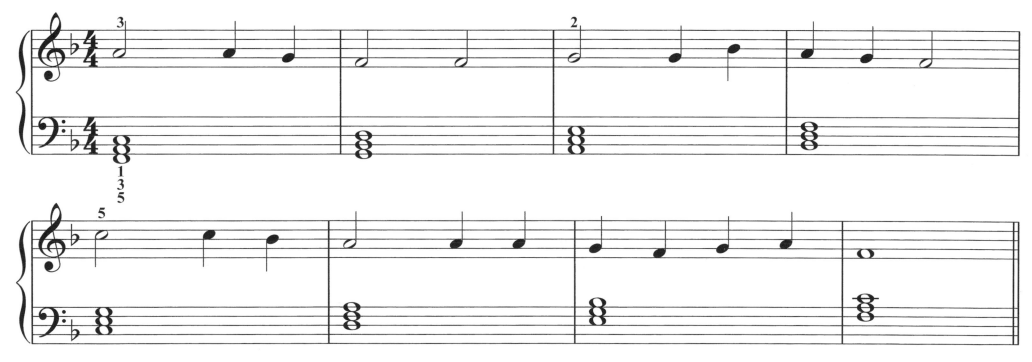

QUESTION AND ANSWER

1. Create both parallel and contrasting Answers. Also transpose up and down to D♭, E♭, and F Major.

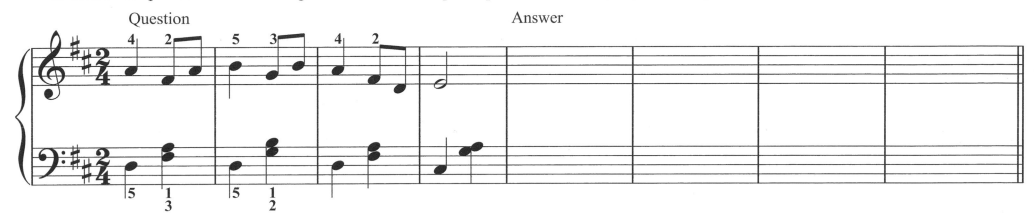

QUESTION AND ANSWER

2. Each day create a new Question followed by different Answers for that Question.

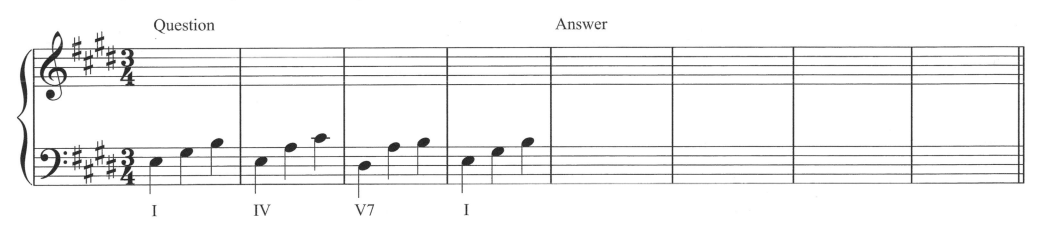

CREATIVE READING

1. For Creative Reading you may change some notes in either hand. Transpose to E and G♭ Major.

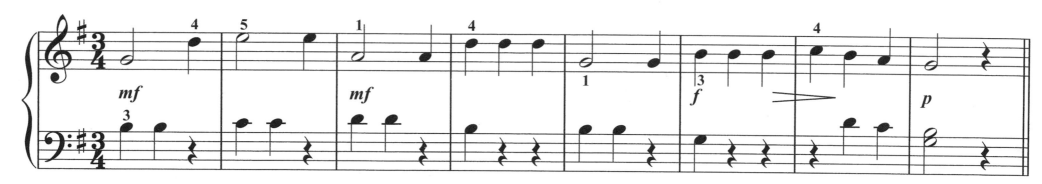

BLUE NOTES

2. Keep the same bass pattern, as you create some new melodic patterns in the right hand.

QUESTION AND ANSWER

1. Create both parallel and contrasting answers each day and make up new questions.

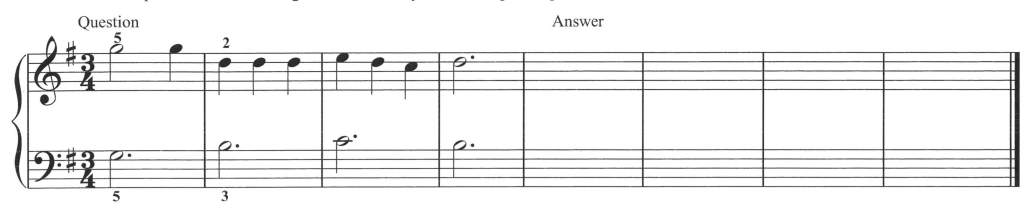

2. Using the blues scale, create new Answers to this Question each day. Also, Create new Questions using the blues scale.

3. Create a new Question and Answer each day and use any of the bass patterns to harmonize them.

Off beat   March   Waltz Bass

RHYTHMIC PATTERNS

1. Chanting "do to do to do" as you play this will help get the correct rhythm. Make up new melodic patterns for Creative Reading.

do to do to do to do

MINOR KEYS

2. Change the melodic patterns for Creative Reading and transpose this to d and e minor.

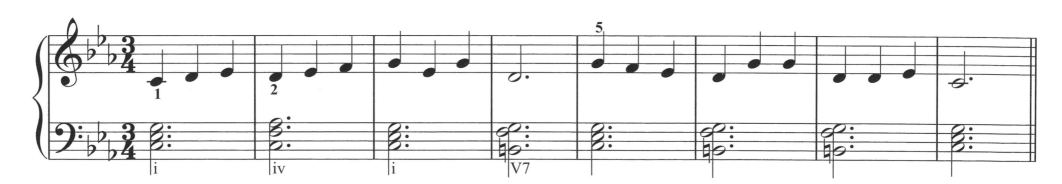

i   iv   i   V7

QUESTION AND ANSWER

1. Use the same bass pattern to create both parallel and contrasting Answers. Also, create your own Question to Answer.

2. Create parallel and contrasting Answers for this Question. Also, create new Questions in minor to Answer.

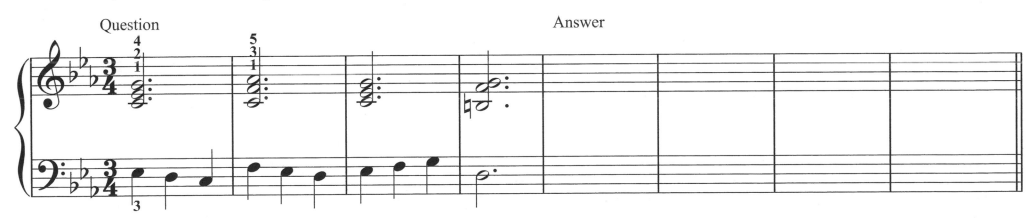

CANON

1. Notice that the right hand imitates the left hand in this Canon. Transpose it to C and E Major.

PHRYGIAN DANCE

2. Play as written, then transpose down one step to play it in Dorian mode.

QUESTION AND ANSWER

1. The right and left hand parts can move in either parallel or contrary motion. Each day create new Answers.

Question   Answer

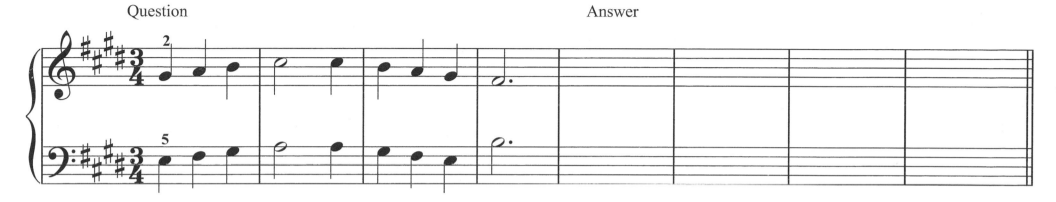

PHRYGIAN QUESTION

2. Create contrasting Answers to this Question, then create other Questions and Answers in Dorian Mode.

Question   Answer

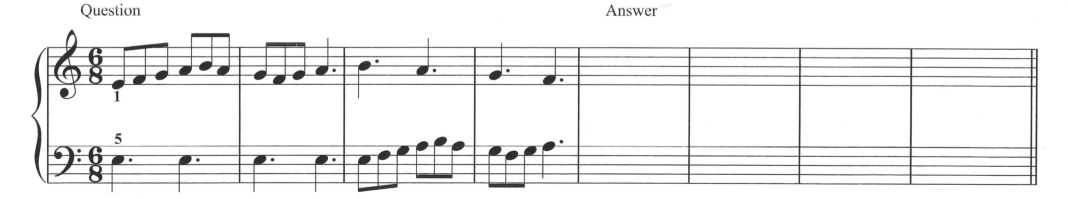

HAYO HAYA

1. First, sightread this as written, then each day try some "Creative Reading" by changing a few notes in the melody.

ANDANTE

2. Transpose this down to D♭ and C Major, then transpose up to E♭ and F Major. Pay special attention to the fingering.

QUESTION AND ANSWER

1. Create both parallel and contrasting Answers to this Question.

ALBERTI BASS

2. Each day create new Answers to this Question using this some Alberti Bass. Also you may make up new Questions using the same bass pattern.

HIGHLAND DANCE

1. Use the same bass pattern and rhythm of the melody to improvise new melodic patterns for your Creative Reading.
   Also transpose this pentatonic tune up and down one half step to play it on all white keys.

RHYTHMIC PATTERNS

2. Think "do to do, to do, to do" to get the rhythm of the melody correct. Transpose to d and f minor.

1. Create new pentatonic Questions and Answers each day.

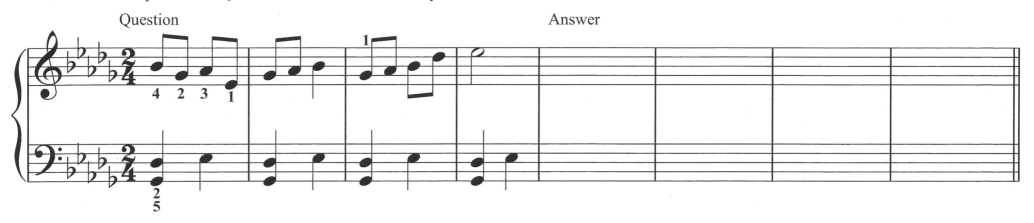

MINOR QUESTIONS AND ANSWERS

2. Improvise new Questions and Answers in the left hand.

OSTINATOS

3. Use these ostinatos to harmonize the melodies for new Questions and Answers.

SURPRISE

1. For Creative Reading keep the same notes in the left hand, and make some changes in the right hand.

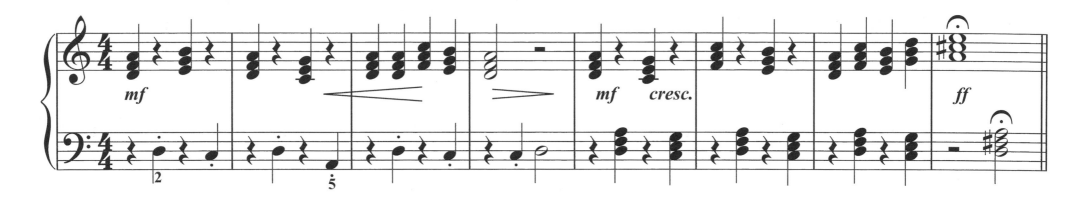

SAILOR'S SONG

2. Change a few notes in the right hand, and transpose to F, E and A♭ Major.

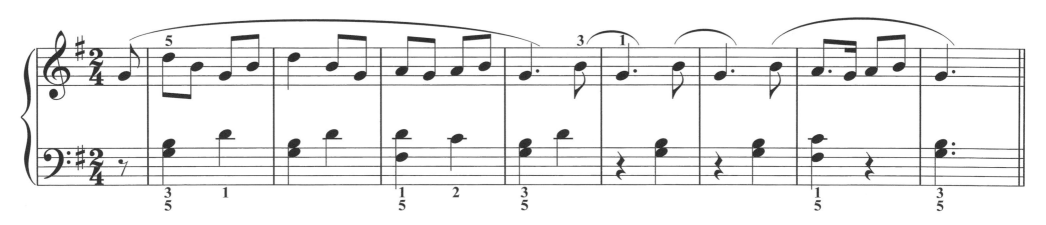

QUESTION AND ANSWER

1. Complete the Answer to this Question, then each day make up new Questions and Answers using a combination of triads and single notes.

Question   Answer

QUESTION AND ANSWER

2. Create a different Answer to this Question each day, and also create your own new Questions. Tranpose to D, D♭ and E♭ Major.

Question   Answer

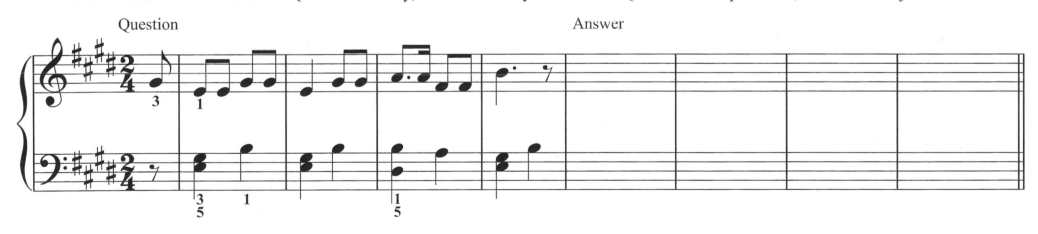

ON YOUR TOES

1. Transpose this down to D♭ and C Major, and up to E♭ and F Major.

ETUDE

2. As you start either the right or left hand scale passage, move your thumb under your third finger immediately to be able to continue the scale without a break. Transpose to C and E Major.

QUESTION AND ANSWER

1. Create both parallel and contrasting Answers for this Question, and make up new Questions in the same style.

Question   Answer

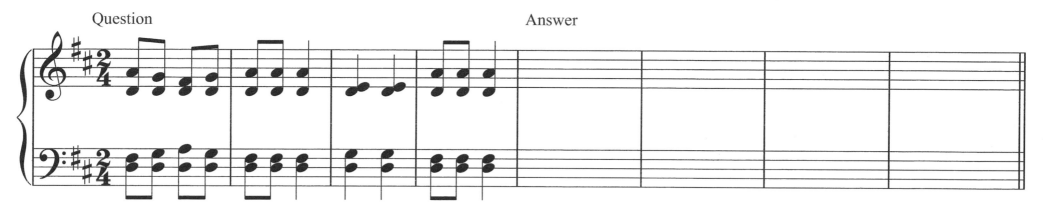

QUESTION AND ANSWER

2. Give both parallel and contrasting Answers, and create new Questions in the same style.

Question   Answer

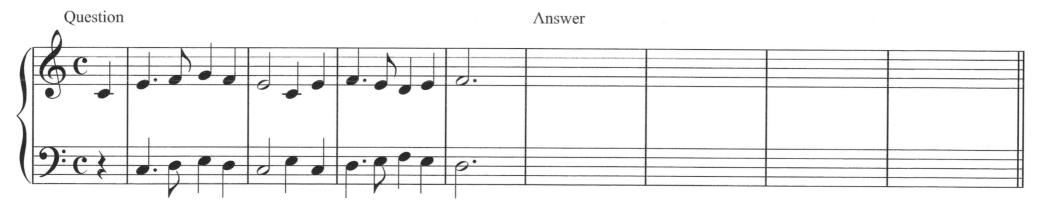

MINUET

1. For Creative Reading, change some of the notes in the right hand melody. The triplet (♪♪♪) in the seventh measure gets the same amount of time as two eighths or one quarter.

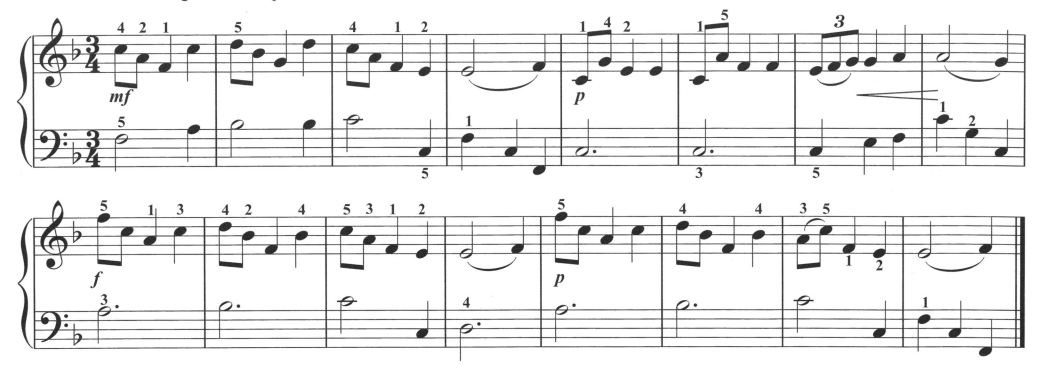

OLD TALE

2. You may change the melody for Creative Reading and transpose down one step to play this in g minor.

QUESTION AND ANSWER

1. Make up both parallel and contrasting Answers to this Question. Also, create your own new Questions to Answer.

QUESTION AND ANSWER

2. Each day Create both parallel and contrasting Answers to this Question. Also, create new Questions to Answer.

MARCH

1. For Creative Reading, you may change either part or both.

MINUET

2. For Creative Reading, change some of the notes in the right hand. Transpose up one whole step to D Major.

MARCH

1. Create one parallel and one contrasting Answer each day and create your own new Questions.

QUESTION AND ANSWER

2. Make up one parallel and one contrasting Answer each day. Also create your own Question in this same style.

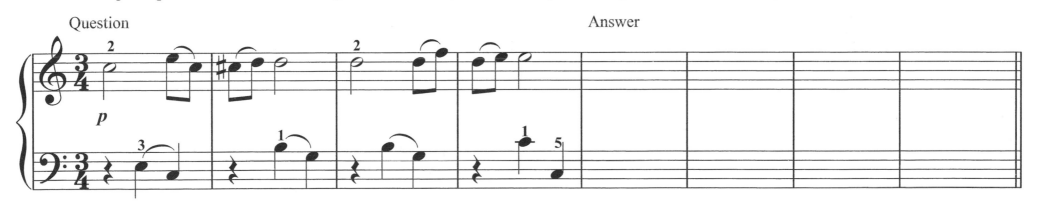

THE CHASE

1. For Creative Reading, begin on the middle tone (third finger) and go up or down. Transpose up one step to D Major.

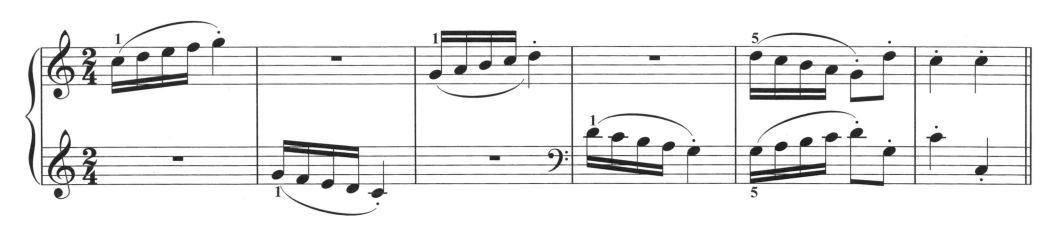

SAILOR'S DANCE

2. Change the direction of the three note melodic figure (♩♪♩.) for Creative Reading.

QUESTION AND ANSWER

1. To create new Questions, begin on either the third or fifth note of the A note figure ().

QUESTION AND ANSWER

2. Make up both parallel and contrasting Answers to this Question, then create new Questions using the same rhythm and harmony.

REVIEW

1. Use the same rhythm but change some of the notes in either hand for Creative Reading. Transpose to E and G Major.

2. Invert the three note figure (♩♪♩) in either hand for Creative Reading. Also, transpose up one step to e minor.

QUESTION AND ANSWER

1. Create both parallel and contrasting Answers for this Question, and make up new Questions to Answer.

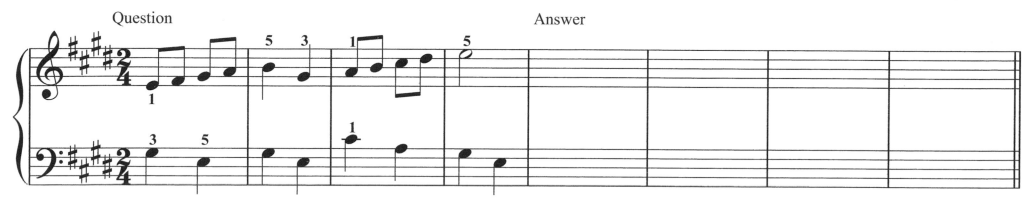

QUESTION AND ANSWER

2. Create both parallel and contrasting Answers for this Question. Use this rhythm to create other Questions and Answers.

2314